Characteristics of Animals

by Libby Romero

Table of Contents

Introduction... 2
Chapter 1 What Are Vertebrates?..................... 4
Chapter 2 What Are Invertebrates?.................. 8
Chapter 3 What Do Animals Need to Live?......... 12
Chapter 4 What Do Animals Do?..................... 16
Summary... 20
Glossary.. 22
Index.. 24

Introduction

Animals are living things. What are the types of animals? Animals live everywhere. How do animals live? Read to learn about animals.

▲ Many animals live in Africa.

Words to Know

 amphibians

 animals

 gills

 invertebrates

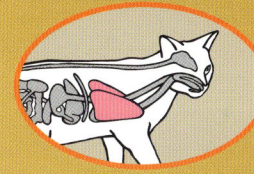 lungs

 mammals

 reptiles

 vertebrates

See the Glossary on page 22.

Chapter 1

What Are Vertebrates?

Some animals are **vertebrates**. Vertebrates have spines. Spines help animals move.

▲ A horse is a vertebrate.

▲ Horses are animals.

Mammals are vertebrates. Female mammals feed milk to baby mammals. Mammals are the only animals with hair.

▲ Cats are mammals.

Chapter 1

Birds are vertebrates. Most birds can fly.

It's a Fact
Birds are the only animals that have feathers.

▲ Penguins are birds.

▲ This bird flies very fast.

Fish are vertebrates, too. Fish live in water.

▲ Sharks are fish.

What Are Vertebrates?

Reptiles are vertebrates with scaly skin. Reptiles get body heat from the sun.

▲ Snakes are reptiles.

Amphibians are vertebrates with moist skin. Amphibians live near water.

▲ Adult frogs live near water.

Chapter 2

What Are Invertebrates?

Some animals are **invertebrates**. Invertebrates do not have spines. Most animals do not have spines. Most animals are invertebrates.

It's a Fact
About 97% of all animals are invertebrates.

▲ Jellyfish are invertebrates.

▲ Jellyfish are animals.

Insects are invertebrates. Most insects have wings.

▲ Insects are invertebrates.

▲ Butterflies are insects with wings.

Chapter 2

Spiders are invertebrates. Spiders have eight legs. Spiders lay eggs. Baby spiders come out of the eggs.

Stop, Think, and Talk

Some animals are vertebrates. Some animals are invertebrates. Think about animals. Talk about which animals are vertebrates. Talk about which animals are invertebrates.

▲ Spiders are invertebrates.

What Are Invertebrates?

Lobsters are invertebrates that live in oceans. Some lobsters have claws.

▲ Lobsters are invertebrates.

Squid are invertebrates. Some people think squid are the smartest invertebrates.

Did You Know?
Sponges are animals. Sponges are invertebrates.

▲ Giant squid are invertebrates.

Chapter 3

What Do Animals Need to Live?

Animals need many things to live. Animals need air to live. Animals breathe oxygen from the air. Some animals use **lungs** to breathe oxygen.

▲ lungs

▲ Tigers use lungs to breathe.

Some animals use **gills** to breathe oxygen. Fish use gills to breathe oxygen.

▲ Gills help fish get oxygen from water.

Did You Know?
Whales look like fish.
Whales are not fish.
Whales are mammals.
Whales use lungs
to breathe.

Chapter 3

Animals need water to live. Animals drink water. Some animals live in the water.

▲ Dogs need water to live.

▲ Crocodiles live mostly in water.

What Do Animals Need to Live?

Animals need food to live. Some animals eat other animals. Some animals eat plants. Some animals eat plants and animals.

▲ Lions eat other animals.

▲ Giraffes eat plants.

▲ People eat plants and animals.

Try This

1. Make a list of what you ate today.
2. Write PLANTS on one side of a paper.
3. Write ANIMALS on the other side.
4. Write the foods under each name.

Chapter 4

What Do Animals Do?

Animals move. Some animals run. Some animals swim. Some animals fly.

▲ A cheetah can run very fast.

▲ An octopus swims.

Solve This

Look at the chart. Which is the fastest animal?

Fast Animals	
Animal	Fastest Speed
blue whale	30 miles per hour (48 kilometers per hour)
cheetah	64 miles per hour (103 kilometers per hour)
dragonfly	60 miles per hour (97 kilometers per hour)
peregrine falcon	200 miles per hour (322 kilometers per hour)
sailfish	68 miles per hour (109 kilometers per hour)

Answer: peregrine falcon

Hungry animals find food. Scared animals run to find safety. Some animals fight.

▲ Animals find food.

▲ Animals run to live.

▲ Some animals fight to live.

Chapter 4

Animals have babies. Birds lay eggs. Fish lay eggs. Most mammals have living babies.

▲ Baby birds are inside these eggs.

▲ Elephants have living babies.

What Do Animals Do?

Animals grow. Animals are many different shapes and sizes.

▲ Giraffes are tall animals.

Did You Know?
The largest bird is the ostrich. Some ostriches grow to be 9 feet (2.7 meters) tall. Some ostriches weigh 345 pounds (156 kilograms).

Summary

Animals are living things. Some animals are vertebrates. Some animals are invertebrates. Animals need many things to live. Animals do many things.

Characteristics of Animals

What Are Vertebrates?
- animals with spines
- mammals
- birds
- fish
- reptiles
- amphibians

What Are Invertebrates?
- animals with no spines
- insects
- spiders
- lobsters
- squid

What Do Animals Do?

move
find food
find safety
fight
have babies
grow

What Do Animals Need to Live?

air
oxygen
water
food

Think About It

1. Which animals are vertebrates?
2. Which animals are invertebrates?
3. What do animals need to live?

Glossary

amphibians vertebrates with moist skin that live in water when young

Amphibians live near water.

animals living things that can move

Animals live everywhere.

gills the body parts fish use to breathe

Fish use gills to breathe oxygen.

invertebrates animals with no spines

Lobsters are invertebrates that live in oceans.

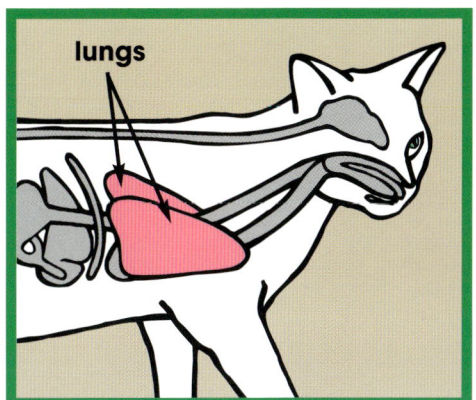

lungs the body parts some animals use to breathe

*Some animals use **lungs** to breathe oxygen.*

mammals vertebrates that feed milk to their babies

***Mammals** are the only animals with hair.*

reptiles animals with scaly skin that lay eggs

***Reptiles** get body heat from the sun.*

vertebrates animals with spines

*Some animals are **vertebrates**.*

Index

air, 12

amphibians, 7

animals, 2, 4–5, 8, 12–20

birds, 6, 18

fight, 17

fish, 6, 13, 18

food, 15, 17

gills, 13

insects, 9

invertebrates, 8–11, 20

lungs, 12

mammals, 5, 18

oxygen, 12–13

reptiles, 7

vertebrates, 4–7, 20

water, 6, 14